Sleep Sound In Jesus

MICHAEL CARD

Illustrated by Catherine McLaughlin

HARVEST HOUSE™ PUBLISHERS

EUGENE, OREGON

Cover by: Terry Dugan Design, Minneapolis, Minnesota
Sleep Sound in Jesus
Copyright © 1990 by The Sparrow Corporation
Published by Harvest House Publishers
Eugene, Oregon 97402
www.harvesthousepublishers.com
Library of Congress Cataloging-in-Publication Data

Card, Michael, 1957-
        Sleep Sound in Jesus / Michael Card.
        ISBN-13: 978-0-7369-1219-8
        ISBN-10: 0-7369-1219-3
        1. Sleep—Religious aspects—Christianity—Meditations.
    I. Title
BV4897.S44C37   1990   89-48732
242—dc20   CIP
Printed in Hong Kong

08 09 10 / NG / 10 9 8 7 6 5

INTRODUCTION

Lullabies come around three times in the course of a lifetime. When we are babies, if we are fortunate, we hear them sung to us by our parents. When we are parents, if we are wise, we sing them to our babies. When we are grandparents, if we are so blessed, we have that last wonderful chance to sing them again as we gaze into a face which reminds us of all our loved ones.

Lullabies are songs we sing to our children and to ourselves. They help express and reinforce our love, acting as tools to bring it to the surface. They remind us of our comforting roles as parents. They are artful ways of loving our children.

Lullabies can also be songs we sing to God. They can be prayers of thanksgiving, petitions for angelic protection, or simple prayers of adoration for the gift of God we are trying to sing to sleep.

At the heart of it all, what lullabies are basically about is *loving*—loving our children and loving God. In these rare moments we know beyond a shadow of a doubt that we are doing exactly the right thing—loving our children and God, and singing simple, sleepy songs to both of them.

—Michael Card

To
Susan
my lullaby-singing partner

CONTENTS

Introduction

Sleep Sound In Jesus

Sleep sound in Jesus my baby, my dear—
Angels are watching, they keep you so near.
Know for His sake you'll be safe for the night;
Sleep sound in Jesus—I'll turn off the light.

Sleep sound in Jesus, sweetheart of my heart;
The dark of the night will not keep us apart.
When I lay you down in your bed for the night
He holds you gently till morning is light.

Sleep sound in Jesus, the angels are here—
They're keeping watch so there's nothing to fear;
Against any foe they are ready to fight
So sleep sound in Jesus—I'll turn off the light.

TO BE "IN JESUS," to be found in Him, whether we are waking or sleeping, is what the Christian life is all about. And if we desire this for ourselves, how much more for our children? But what does being "in Jesus" really mean? Many of us describe the experience of coming to faith by saying, "I've asked Jesus into my heart." Our perspective is that it is Jesus who is in us. And of course that is true, for His Spirit dwells within us. This is a profound realization for the new Christian. Yet the New Testament more often speaks of our being "in Christ."

"In Him we live and move and have our being." We are to be wrapped in Him, hidden in Him, found in Him. What these expressions say to us is that beyond asking Jesus to come into our hearts, we must come to the staggering realization that Jesus wants to invite us into His life, into His heart. To be "in Him" means to have accepted His invitation to live out our lives in His life. This is our greatest hope for the children with which we have been gifted—that they will come to live their lives "in Jesus," that they will find themselves "in Him."

He'll Wipe Away Your Tears

From our mother's first soft lullaby
We sing and we weep and we know not why
That as sons of the earth from our first cry
We weep to show we are alive.

He'll wipe away your tears
And still your restless sighs
And lovingly He'll listen till
You stop your wordless cries.

He'll wipe away your tears
By the hand within my hand.
The Lord who knows of tears so well
Must surely understand—

And so when He returns again
To wake us from the sleep of sin
The Lord who now regards your cry
Will gently see each tear is dried.

*T*EARS ARE A MYSTERY. They are the first indication that we are alive. They are present both when we weep and when we laugh. They are a shining bridge between sorrow and joy, glistening at both. And while there are usually reasons for our tears, there is something about them which is still a mystery.

Babies have the amazing ability to cause us to shift our focus from our own tears to theirs. And as parents we spend a good deal of time dealing with the different causes of their tears. If it were possible, we would erase every one of them. But that is not possible, and often we are left simply holding our children, comforting them in this fallen and tear-filled world.

Sometimes the best we can do is simply wipe their tears away—which in itself is a wondrous thing to do when we stop and think about it. For it is Jesus Himself who twice promises to do the same thing for us someday. To recognize His hand within our hand as we wipe away our children's tears is to begin to understand the truth that through us He begins to fulfill that promise.

Even the Darkness Is Light to Him
From Psalm 139

*Even the darkness is light to Him
And night is as bright as the day,
So you are safe though the light grows dim
For even the darkness is light to Him.*

*The Father above does not slumber or sleep,
He wakefully watches our ways.
Then there's no reason for you to weep
For the Father above does not slumber or sleep.*

*So dry your eyes of angel blue
And trust the One who died for you.
Would not Jesus safely keep
The little ones He loves asleep?*

PSALM 139 IS A POEM to the God who searches and knows our hearts. David, overcome by this realization, could only respond, "Such knowledge is too wonderful for me!" And he was right—it is wonderful to be known so completely by such a God.

Jesus reveals a God whose total knowledge of us we need not fear, for God is love and He is light. He loves us as we are and not as we should be. Fickle human love is based on reasons. But God needs no reasons to love; He *is* love! And because His love is not based on reasons, it cannot change—not until He changes, and He never does!

He is also light. Therefore fear, which is really only one form of darkness, simply cannot exist before Him. "If we walk with Him, we walk in the light, for He is the light." If we find ourselves in the darkness, whether spiritual or physical, we must trust Him as we remember that He is still the light.

As we entrust our little ones and ourselves to His care when we are most vulnerably asleep, we take comfort in knowing that the darkness around us is really light to Him. And when deep darkness seems to surround our hearts, we know that God is not only *the* light but that through Christ Jesus He is *our* light.

Sweet Sleep Descends

It breaks my heart to see the woe
My little one must undergo
To fume and fuss and whine and weep
At simply laying down to sleep.

She scorns the angel of repose,
Tries every tactic that she knows
And fights it till the bitter end
Until at last sweet sleep descends.

Throughout the house of faith it's known
The soul finds rest in God alone,
That He grants sleep to those He loves
Yet slumbers not, nor sleeps above.

DAVID WAS A TIRED OLD MAN when he wrote Psalm 62. He referred to himself as a "leaning wall," and he certainly had every reason to feel like one. The family of Saul was trying to pull down David and everything he had accomplished during his tiring and tumultuous reign. David was a tired man, desperately seeking rest. But despite the tumult and distractions, or perhaps because of them, David made a wonderful discovery: True rest is not the absence of turmoil. He discovered that true rest is found not in a *place* but in a *Person*. He put it this way: "My soul finds rest in God alone." David's God, who Himself rested on the Sabbath, is the only source of true rest.

In the closing stanzas of the song, David states his two reasons for finding his rest in God alone: "One thing God has spoken, two things I have heard: that you, O God, are strong, and that you, O Lord, are loving." It is the combination of God's strength and love which make Him the truest source of rest. He Himself is our rest.

That's what singing lullabies is all about—true rest. And the Lord is the giver of this true rest, whether you are a weary old king or a tired newborn.

Dreaming Jacob's Dream

Are you dreaming Jacob's dream?
Could that be why you're smiling?
Could you not be a man like he,
So wily and beguiling?

Jacob dreamed about Someone,
A Way to heaven, God the Son,
And someday it's my prayer for you
That in your heart his dream comes true.

Do you see a ladder there
Reaching up to heaven?
Do the angels fill the air?
Could you reach out and touch them?

You do not sleep upon a stone,
You have a bed to lay in,
But you and Jacob aren't alone—
We all need dreams to seek Him.

Some of our dreams may come from God, but more often they concern themselves with things we want to accomplish. We dream of building this house or taking that trip. If only our dreams could be more like Jacob's, who dreamed of what *God* would do!

What Jacob's dream revealed about God is really staggering: a ladder with one end resting on the earth and the other end in the clouds of heaven—in other words, a way to heaven.

In the Gospel of John, Jesus referred to this dream of Jacob's and in no uncertain terms identified Himself as the wonderful ladder. It was His way of saying that Jacob's dream had finally come true!

We must pray that our dreams will be transformed in such a way, that they will change from what we want to do to what God wants to do in us and in our children. And what He wants to do in us can be clearly seen in Jacob's dream: God wants us to see the Way, to climb up that way to Him, that way whose name is Jesus!

Song of Jesus

Let me tell you of a Man
Who was before the world began,
Who loves you more than anyone can,
Known by the name of Jesus.

If He could cause the storm to clear
He'll calm the tempest of your tears;
If He could cause the dead to rise
At dawn He'll open up your eyes.

He was born a babe like you
And every word He spoke is true.
I pray you'll come to know Him too
And live your life for Jesus.

So rest your weary head tonight
And dream of Him who is the Life
And wake up to His world of Light
And sing the name of Jesus.

BEING A PARENT involves nurturing our children. While providing food and shelter is basic and important, feeding them the True Bread is the highest purpose and responsibility for a parent.

This involves simply telling them about Jesus. But telling is not always easy, for telling involves using not only your lips but your life as well. If you have told them that Jesus is love but have not yourself been a loving person, you have contradicted yourself. If you speak to them of Jesus' healing power but fail to heal their hurts, you have only confused the issue. Telling your children about Jesus with your life is the most powerful message they can receive. It is serious business.

The telling that takes place through the lips is truly Christ calling out to our children through us. It is a joy and a wonder. It is a mystery. But even greater is the mystery that takes place when Christ calls to us through our children. As we speak to them about Him, He sometimes speaks to us too, and calls us to be with Him in the present moment, where all children live. And so through our children God calls us to become children again as well, and bids us come to Him.

Unseen Warriors

Oh, unseen warriors, brothers, friends,
Who for our safety we depend,
I ask you now to come defend
This precious little baby.

I know you've been here all along
And will remain her whole life long,
But with this simple childish song
I ask you, guard this baby.

Sometimes at night she will awaken,
Let her not feel fear forsaken.
To every saint your visit paid
You always said, "Don't be afraid."

WITH VERY FEW EXCEPTIONS, when angels appear in the Bible, the first words they speak are, "Don't be afraid." There are a lot of things to be afraid of in this world, and that's exactly why God has assigned angels to help us.

They are often seen with swords because they do a lot of fighting. They have individual names and probably individual personalities, because they are both persons and individuals. They are endowed with power and wisdom to guard us effectively. They are tempted, because at one point a number of them fell and followed Satan, himself once an angel. Don't you suppose they get discouraged with the difficult task they've been given? You can imagine them wondering "When will this struggle ever end?" Their struggle is not only with the devil and his demons, but also with us and the way we are. That's enough to tire and discourage anyone, even an angel!

Given all this, perhaps we should add these unseen warriors to our prayers—not to pray *to* them but *for* them. The angel that God has placed at your side is your keeper and friend; he watches and cares for you even as you read these very words.

Wordless Ones

In Your loving arms we lay
These wordless ones so new;
The incarnation of our love
We dedicate to You.

Hopeless yet so full of hope
We make a solemn vow,
Not knowing when their time will come,
Not even knowing how.
And though it seems we try and make
A promise that is true
We really only claim for them
The Promise that is You.

The holy sleep that falls so deep,
A blessing from above,
Will now embrace our little one
In simple trusting love.
We offer You this child
Who's only ours for just awhile;
How could we keep it back from You
When You gave Your only Child?

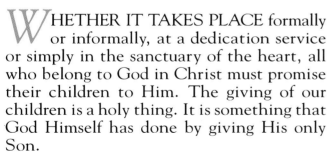

WHETHER IT TAKES PLACE formally or informally, at a dedication service or simply in the sanctuary of the heart, all who belong to God in Christ must promise their children to Him. The giving of our children is a holy thing. It is something that God Himself has done by giving His only Son.

When we dedicate a child to the Lord, many things happen at once. Our children become part of a covenant we make with God. It is still left to them to accept Christ into their lives at some point, but now they are part of something that will shape their lives. We have placed Christ before them as their goal.

The dedication of an infant has just as significant an impact on the parents as on the child, perhaps more. For they too become part of a covenant and a promise. They pledge to take on the task of raising the child to know Jesus. And as the world rages against them, that becomes an increasingly difficult task. In dedicating their baby they are at the same time dedicating themselves. They give the incarnation of their love to God as He has given the Incarnation of His love to them.

He Grants Sleep to Those He Loves

Today was so full
And so busy for both of us
But for tonight all those burdens
  can keep.
Come, let sweet Jesus be the
  Light in your darkness
And open the door to the
  paradise of sleep.

For He grants sleep to the
  ones that He loves
And I live to love you as well.
The last words you'll hear
  tonight will be "I love you,"
For love takes us all a lifetime
  to tell.

Your tender sadness, it touches the heart of me;
Howling and scowling just make you more dear.
With all this commotion now what could the trouble be?
For love's sake, my darling, I'll always be here.

ANYONE WHO HAS BEEN FORCED to go without sleep for a long time will tell you that sleep is a gift. And Solomon certainly had many sleepless nights by the time he wrote Psalm 127!

Like most of God's gifts, sleep is a mystery. Science has probed it for years, but has only come up with a few wiggly lines on a piece of graph paper. Poets have tried to write about sleep, but the best thing they've come up with yet is something about a raveled sleeve. Jesus used it as a metaphor for being dead. And if you look at someone who is sound asleep, you understand what He was talking about. Sleep is a mystery that is better left unsolved.

It is enough to realize what a blessing sleep is: God graciously grants it to us because we need it as much as food or air, that to be asleep is to be embraced as a mystery.

Lullabies are a way of hurrying this mystery along, which in itself is a pretty mysterious thing to do. (Most mysteries take their own sweet time.) They usher our little ones into the arms of the mystery of sleep, into the arms of God Himself.

Jesus, Let Us Come to Know You

Jesus, let us
Come to know You,
Let us see You
Face to face.
Touch us, hold us,
Use us, mold us—
Only let us
Live in You.

Jesus, draw us
Ever nearer,
Hold us in Your
Loving arms.
Wrap us in Your
Gentle presence
And when the end comes
Bring us home.

EVEN PAUL, WHO WAS AS CLOSE to Jesus as anyone, broke down at one point with the desperate cry, "I want to know Christ!" (Philippians 3:10). Who hasn't felt envy at reading John's words, "what our hands have touched" (1 John 1:1)? Knowing Christ is not merely the most important issue; it is the *only* issue, since knowing Him is eternal life (John 17:3).

Those of us who have a saving knowledge of Jesus often describe that experience by saying, "I know Jesus." But what do we mean when we say that? In the Bible we read about Jesus, but knowing facts about Him isn't the same thing as knowing Him personally. We call ourselves by His name, but that is not what it means to know Him either. I know some people who are Calvinists, but that doesn't mean they ever knew John Calvin personally.

We primarily come to know people by speaking to them. Once we begin to speak with someone we often draw closer, perhaps even to embrace or be embraced by them. But first we talk and we listen. And that is what prayer is all about: speaking and listening to Jesus, and waiting expectantly to feel His embrace.

All You Are

Where did you get those eyes so blue?
They're from the sky that you passed through.
Where did you get that little tear?
Did you find that it was waiting for you here?

For all you are and all you'll be,
For everything you mean to me,
Though I don't understand,
I know you're from the Father's hand.

And what about your little nose?
He knew you'd need it for the rose.
And as for your soft curly ear,
He knew there would be songs for you to hear.

How can it be that you are you?
He thought you up and so you grew.
Because you're mine it must be true
That He was also thinking of me too.

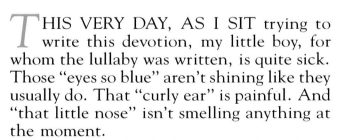

THIS VERY DAY, AS I SIT trying to write this devotion, my little boy, for whom the lullaby was written, is quite sick. Those "eyes so blue" aren't shining like they usually do. That "curly ear" is painful. And "that little nose" isn't smelling anything at the moment.

Though I should be aware of it all the time, it is at moments like these that I realize what a tremendous gift children are, what a blessing from the Lord. When God gives a gift He wraps it in a person, whether it is a baby, or a poor person, or Jesus Himself. Babies are gifts from the Father's hand; He designed them especially for us (Psalm 139:13).

It is miraculous to receive something from God's hand, to realize that He was the source, the giver. So why do we waste time looking for other miracles, even concocting them? We need to pray for eyes to see that it is our *children* who are the miracles. God was not only thinking about *them* when He was creating, but He was also thinking about *us*. He was excited at the thought of giving us such a wonderful gift. So embrace your child as a miraculous gift, and never confuse the gift with the Giver.

Lullaby for the Unborn

Blessings upon you,
My baby unborn,
Safely inside me
Asleep and so warm.
Sleep must come easy
To those who are unborn,
As the Maker so silently
Fashions your form.

Sleep while you can now,
So watery and warm,
For outside this world
Is a terrible storm.
Soon you'll discover
The taste of your tears,
So sleep now, my loved one,
My baby, my dear.

MOST OF US ARE GIVEN nine months to prepare for the impossible task of being parents. Thankfully, the One who gives us this impossible task is also the God of grace who gives us impossible power. During that preparatory time our thoughts become focused on a dark and mysterious place. David went so far as to call it "the secret place" (Psalm 139:15).

Though it may remain a secret place to us, nothing is kept secret from God. Jeremiah was told that God knew him while he was still in the womb (Jeremiah 1:5). There was a purpose and a plan for his life even before he was born. And the same is true for each of us.

Yet those involved in waiting for a baby know what this world can be like. We know that sometimes God's plan includes suffering, and it is hard for us to envision pain in the future for anyone, especially our unborn.

More certain than suffering, however, is the knowledge that God desires everyone to come to Him, that being born is only meant to be a prelude to being born again. This is our comfort as we stand at the door of that "secret place," waiting to see who God will send for us to love.

Sleepy Eyes

Sleepy eyes,
Baby cries,
You're too small to wonder why.
Wrap the band of slumber
'Round your sleepy eyes.

Won't you cease
And just release
And stop this hopeless
*   fighting, please?*

Sleepy eyes,
Tired sighs,
Yawning as the daylight dies—
Sleep won't dim the dawn inside
Those sleepy eyes.

Sleepy eyes,
Your disguise
Cannot fool me with its lies;
Let the angels come and close
Your sleepy eyes.

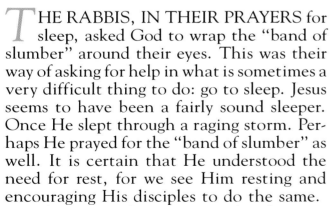

THE RABBIS, IN THEIR PRAYERS for sleep, asked God to wrap the "band of slumber" around their eyes. This was their way of asking for help in what is sometimes a very difficult thing to do: go to sleep. Jesus seems to have been a fairly sound sleeper. Once He slept through a raging storm. Perhaps He prayed for the "band of slumber" as well. It is certain that He understood the need for rest, for we see Him resting and encouraging His disciples to do the same.

I have never been very good at sleeping. My daughter is just the same. We can always find something better to do. Rest, in one form or another, is something we all fight. But rest is part of God's plan, part of His provision for us. If rest is so important to God, then why is it of so little importance to us?

As parents we are quick to recognize what happens to our children when they haven't had their rest: They are not themselves. And perhaps that is why rest is so important for all of us. Maybe God wants to use it in our lives as parents to help us "be ourselves," or at least be the self He wants us to become.

Hold Me Gently

Hold me gently in your arms
As I drift away to sleep;
Wrap the band of slumber round my eyes
As his watch my angel keeps.

Please be there with me
To greet the day;
Always there with me
To show the way;
Live your life within me
Day by day.
So goodnight, my forever Friend.

"THE ONE THING we absolutely owe to God is never to be afraid of anything," Charles deFocauld once said. But most often we are motivated by fear and not by confidence in God. He is not seen as a friend, when in fact He is the one true Friend. Jesus called us friends in an incredible gesture of intimacy. So if we have reason to doubt the power of our own prayers, perhaps we can learn to trust the sufficiency of the prayers of Jesus, for He is both Savior and Friend, and He prays for us.

Escaping our fear is not a matter of denying the danger, for this world is certainly a fearful and fallen place. The exodus from our fear is *Jesus Himself*. It is He who prays for us, who sends angels to guard us, who gave His own life so that we might live our lives without fear. It is Jesus Christ who possesses the absolute power to protect and defend and who loves us beyond measure. If we need not be afraid of Him, we need not be afraid of anything, for Jesus, the Lord of power, is also our Friend.

Barocha
From Numbers 6:24-26

The Lord bless you and keep you,
The Lord make His face shine upon you
And give you peace,
And give you peace,
And give you peace forever.

The Lord be gracious to you,
The Lord turn His face towards you
And give you peace,
And give you peace,
And give you peace forever.

A BAROCHA OR "BLESSING" in Hebrew culture was something of great value. It was a word that carried with it prophetic meaning. So coveted was this word that someone like Jacob would even try to steal it.

We see the crowds bringing children to Jesus so that He might impart His barocha on them. It was Jesus' habit to pronounce blessings.

Blessings are important because they are made up of words, and words are important because they have power. They somehow involve the essence of what it means to be human. That's why when Jesus becomes incarnate He is called the Word. So the words that make up our blessings must be carefully and prayerfully chosen.

Until we become familiar with blessing our children, it is best to use the words that God has provided for blessing them. And Numbers 6 is the best example. God gave it to Aaron to bless his sons. It is a wonderful thing to close the evening with this blessing. To paraphrase Frederick Buechner, blessings are not just words that are true; they are words that make us true.

Lullaby for the Innocents

Hear now a lullaby
You'll never hear,
For your life was something
That wasn't held dear.
You need not a lullaby
For you do not weep,
Nor love's arms to hold you—
In death you do sleep.

What your life might have been
We'll never know;
A miracle happened
But there's nothing to show.
We're left with this sorrow
But hope all the same
In heaven there's Someone
Who knows you by name.